HEAD OF RESEARCH
My Ten-Year Roller-Coaster Ride on Wall Street

Yi Chen

YCX Press

Head of Research: My Ten-Year Roller-Coaster Ride on Wall Street
Copyright © 2011 Yi Chen
Published by YCX Press

All rights reserved. No part of this book may be reproduced (except for inclusion in reviews), disseminated or utilized in any form or by any means, electronic or mechanical, including photocopying, recording, or in any information storage and retrieval system, or the Internet/World Wide Web without written permission from the author or publisher.

For more information visit www.iamthefutures.com

Book design by:

Arbor Books, Inc.
www.arborbooks.com

Printed in the United States of America

Head of Research: My Ten-Year Roller-Coaster Ride on Wall Street
Yi Chen

1. Title   2. Author   3. Memoir

Library of Congress Control Number: 2011907803

ISBN 13: 978-0-6154880-9-7

TABLE OF CONTENTS

NOTE TO THE READER v

CHAPTER 1   One Crazy Day 1

CHAPTER 2   Goldman Sachs 11

CHAPTER 3   Entering the Jungle 15

CHAPTER 4   Life in a Fortress 25

CHAPTER 5   Taking a Step Back 39

CHAPTER 6   Climbing the Turret, Part I 49

CHAPTER 7   Climbing the Turret, Part II 57

CHAPTER 8   The Imperial Bank, Part I 69

CHAPTER 9   The Imperial Bank, Part II 81

CHAPTER 10   The Aftermath 93

CHAPTER 11   Rising from the Ashes 101

NOTE TO THE READER

This book is the story of my life as a Wall Street quantitative analyst and portfolio manager. I worked for the some of the most successful banks and investment firms the world has to offer and through hard work and determination, I earned promotions and accolades. I also learned that not everything we want in life can be ours. I also learned valuable lessons from the setbacks I suffered and I became a stronger person because of those setbacks.

Some of the names of the banks I worked for and the people I worked with have been changed to protect their reputations. The political infighting and competition for income on Wall Street can be aggressive but I don't want to paint anyone in a bad light. The facts of what happened and the conversations portrayed are accurate to the best of my memories.

I want to thank all of the people who supported me in my time of need over the last year. The outpouring of emotional support and comfort has been overwhelming and it has kept me strong and given me the motivation to move forward with my life.

Last but not least I want to thank my wife and my daughter. They are the center of my life and have given me great moments of joy amidst the heartache I've felt in my career.

—Yi Chen

CHAPTER 1

One Crazy Day

I climbed the last few stairs out of the subway station and into the dense morning air on Broadway in New York City. Throngs of morning commuters pushed past me, splitting the haze hanging between the city's buildings. The heat clung to the commuters, weighing them down and adding another burden to a nightmare summer. It was August 2007, and the financial collapse was hitting full stride.

Ten minutes away, my office awaited. As a portfolio manager at a large hedge fund, I was acutely aware of the madness traveling through the financial system and what it meant for each commuter's 401(k) or college fund. But few people outside of the industry seemed to understand how bad things were getting.

You could tell the financial industry insiders from the normal commuters because the insiders looked like they were harboring a terrible secret. Their postures gave away the burden they were carrying, and their sullen eyes spoke of the late nights they spent scrambling to cover losses in the market.

Head of Research

Some of the financial workers were harboring a secret. The general public didn't know at the time just how desperate the financial picture was beginning to look as sub-prime–backed assets imploded throughout the world's economy. They saw some headlines and heard about a few large firms in trouble, but does anyone with a full-time job in another industry really know what goes on behind closed doors on Wall Street?

I knew, and so did many of my fellow travelers that morning, and that's why so many of us rushed through the morning heat to our offices. My pace was quickened by the fact that life for me was always hectic, and I had developed the attitude of a soldier at war.

My tenure on Wall Street was just seven years old, and in that time things had gone from smooth sailing to fighting every day for my job. The jungle had closed in around me, and I was among animals, fiercely protecting myself and looking for a way up through the canopy to the dream jobs above.

I wanted the million-dollar payday that all of us craved; it was the next step in a plan I'd formed as a teenager in China where fighting for grades and a position at a good university had hardened me for my life ahead.

I pushed through the front door of our high-rise building on Broadway and rode silently up to the 10th floor. It was 7:45, but the trading floor, which occupied an entire corner of the building, was already buzzing, especially where my group sat.

One Crazy Day

I worked for the The Newton Group, ten people under the umbrella of Fortress Investment, a famous macro hedge fund employing a few hundred traders and analysts divided up into specialist groups and managing about $7 billion in capital. I could see from across the floor as I approached my teammates that they and especially Raj, my direct boss and the senior-most portfolio manager, were absolutely panicked.

His face was pallid—bleached, even. He stared at the screens in front of him, reviewing some of our strategies and the numbers from the previous week. They weren't good. In fact, they were terrifying.

In mid-February of that year we had been up $20 million and were flying high, congratulating ourselves on our grand successes. It was so easy to make money in 2006 and in the early part of 2007 that the stock market had hit a record high just weeks before Raj's face turned white.

Our group was fairly new at Fortress, but in 2006 we had made $15 million. Then, with our February 2007 haul of $20 million, we were fist pumping and dreaming of a $100 million year.

That dream, however, lay shattered on the floor around Raj's feet.

Just as I reached my desk, Doug, the head honcho in our group, approached Raj. "Raj, what's going on with these numbers?"

Raj shook his head and turned to Doug. "The end of the world." He was shaken, and like most of us in the business, the market just seemed like an episode of *The Twilight Zone*. When I saw his face, my heart dropped a little. I wanted to keep my job; I wanted some stability in my career. That day would give me a sense of stability, but it didn't guarantee any safety in my career.

That Friday, August 17th, might as well have been the end of the world. We were hemorrhaging money at more than $1 million a day, erasing the profits we'd collected that year. It felt surreal and a world away from that January. We were down more than $10 million, the direct opposite of the start of the year.

I took my seat and dove into my research for the day. I was running about $100 million of risk capital in my book, and I was doing well considering the circumstances. I was determined to help the team, but my contributions were being swallowed by a sea of losses. As the sub-prime mortgage mess spread around the globe, positions long believed stable were collapsing.

Our group was in one of these positions, having bought, or gone long, the Japanese Yen and having sold, or gone short, the Australian dollar, famously known as "currency carry trade." It was reversing on us that week, and we were looking for a way to shift our long-term strategies. My job was to pore through our strategies one by one to find ways to bolster our positions.

Analysis and investigation are my real talents, and over the previous week I'd found a few bright spots in our

One Crazy Day

positions to help navigate safe passage through this nightmare market. I had been in the office until 2 that morning, returning home to shower and grab a few hours' sleep before turning around and heading back in. I was making some progress, and Raj was grateful. He came to my desk to see how I was doing.

"Yi, we better hope this works."

I wish it had, but it was too late. As the trading day really got going, the normal rhythm and hum of the place just wasn't there. The noise on the floor was muted; I wasn't hearing the sharp sounds I usually heard during a normal trading day—the yelling was more hostile, the questions more confused, and the attitude more desperate.

The haze from outside seemed to creep indoors, dampening the spirits of the traders and masking any future recovery. As a member of a hedge fund you accept that there will be risk, but even when you're down, there is a constant hope that the losses would reverse themselves and that you could crawl your way into profitability with savvy trading.

This, however, was different.

The looks on people's faces said it all. This time we didn't know when we were going to get it back. For the first time in years, after making money at an alarming rate, the traders at Fortress saw the possibility that it could all come crashing down, and this time for good.

The risk manager for the firm sat five chairs down

from me, and I could see all of the problems from the firm's groups landing in his lap that morning. His eyes were bloodshot and his tie was loose. He looked worse than Raj, and as the day went on, the look on his face just kept getting worse.

Rumors had been circulating since June that two of Bear Sterns' hedge funds were on the brink of being seized by creditors, namely Merrill Lynch. It had sold off $4 billion in assets already, but it wasn't enough, and it was looking for a way out of the sub-prime mess. We didn't own sub-prime–backed assets, but when one ship sinks on Wall Street, the others sink too.

Just as Raj turned toward his desk, one of the firm's senior partners made his way down our aisle.

"Guys, gather around here for a minute."

Jeff, who sat next to me, turned toward me and shrugged his shoulders. Senior partners rarely came across the floor from their glass-walled offices to speak with the traders. I shrugged back, and we both turned our chairs to face him.

"I know you guys have had a rough week; hell, everybody has. I just want you to know that you're not alone in this. We've been checking around, and it's been an awful week for everyone. Even the best are struggling to catch up to these changes. Don't worry—we'll get it figured out, and the market will rebound." He mentioned that Two

One Crazy Day

Sigma Investments, still one of the best quantitative hedge funds out there, had recently had its worst day since inception.

As he walked back to his office, Jeff looked at Raj. "Okay. Now I know we're screwed. No one gives a talk like that unless he's petrified."

Raj barely looked up from his desk. I went back to work, trying to figure out how to save us from complete collapse and hoping that somehow we would find a way forward. I believe that in these moments in my career, when everything was on the line, I showed what I was made of. Persevering that day was all I could do, and so that's what I did, making quick decisions.

In the midst of the madness there were so many issues to deal with. We were reevaluating our own strategies and also watching the markets unravel as hedge fund after hedge fund liquidated positions automatically as their safety stops, or orders to sell if a price fell below a certain level, were reached. But I was able to analyze and pinpoint inefficiencies in our currency model, and I went to Doug with my findings.

He was happy but skeptical. He wanted someone else to review them, and so Jeff stepped in and started checking my work. Jeff was Doug's golden boy at Goldman Sachs, and his look at my work doubled as a grab for credit where it wasn't due. I knew what he was doing, but when you don't have a patron on Wall Street, sometimes you have to keep your mouth shut. Besides, my work was going to have to wait. Doug was panicked.

That afternoon around 3, I overheard Doug talking to Raj. "I think we need to just get out for a while."

"Do you mean liquidate?" Raj asked, his voice cracking.

"Yeah. I don't think we have any choice."

Liquidating our positions, fleeing the markets, was a move of last resort. We had already bought more positions as the prices fell, hoping that they would bounce back. But they were…deep in the red as well. Dumping it all would cost us millions and set us back for the entire year. But as Raj had said so many times in the previous week, "This just isn't a normal market."

Doug huddled with Raj, Jeff, and me and reviewed our options. We didn't really have any. There are positions in the financial markets to which all large hedge funds flock, and when those go down, it's every man for himself. When our Japanese Yen/Australian Dollar position hit the skids, we all knew it was time to find shelter.

By day's end we had decided to pull out. As I walked down Broadway toward the subway station I dragged my feet, drained from the exertion of the day but buoyed by our efforts. I could tell that things had gotten worse at other firms because the commuters who had shared my train in the morning were heading home and looking worse for the wear.

One Crazy Day

Days later we pulled out of the market for a week, sheltering ourselves from further losses.

It was just another day during my roller-coaster ride on Wall Street.

CHAPTER 2

Goldman Sachs

On days like August 17, 2007, I sometimes looked back at my road to New York and the bright lights of the financial world. I was born in China, an only child like so many others there, and I had climbed my way up through China's fiercely competitive school system. At one point I ranked third in the national school physics competition, one of many academic accomplishments for the competitive, driven kid I was.

I was accepted by Tsinghua University, the MIT of China, without having to take an entrance exam. It was a huge honor for my family and part of a smooth, almost dreamlike rise up the ranks in my youth. In fact, before I arrived at Tsinghua, I didn't really know what it meant to fail or to feel ordinary.

I had been treated as a star in high school, and I was confident. But my confidence was quickly shattered in college. There is a very unbalanced educational system in China: there are fewer famous colleges than there are top-notch high schools. I quickly realized that all of the students there were equally as good as I was. We had some guys who had ranked at the top in their college entrance exams, and several other guys who had done very well in the national physics or math competitions.

The competition at Tsinghua was fierce. I couldn't dream of being in the top five in my classes as I had done so easily in high school. At Tsinghua I was forced to accept the fact that there were students better than I was in my subjects.

I managed to pass most of my courses by working hard for a few days before final exams. I had to work hard in those days because I actually skipped many of my classes to focus on learning computer programming (and to play a few games).

By the time I graduated, I was fielding offers from various PhD programs, and I chose the University of Pennsylvania because its Wharton School of Business is at the heart of the business world. I would get my PhD in physics but always with an eye toward business.

It wasn't uncommon for Chinese students to go to the United States for graduate work, but I also had visions of a life a little more glamorous than that. I wanted to make my millions on Wall Street, and I set about doing just that.

To apply my physics knowledge to the business world, I spent my last six months at Penn studying various option theories and C++ programming language books because I knew that quantitative analysts on Wall Street used those tools in their work. And then I set off to find my first job.

Goldman Sachs

I eventually landed one at the Quantitative Strategy group at Goldman Sachs. The group is famous because it was originally headed by Emanual Derman, an ex-physicist who pioneered local volatility models in derivative pricing in the financial markets. Most of the guys in that group were ex-physicists, so we had a lot in common.

I was pretty lucky to land a job where I did, but I also accomplished a lot in a short period of time. Our group was responsible for the exotic derivative pricing library and risk system that Goldman used, and we were making a name for ourselves. I was lucky that soon after I joined the group, part of the "quants," as we were called, split off from the main group and moved to the front-office trading desk on the top floor of One New York Plaza.

I was now in the center of the equity derivative trading floor at Goldman. Big equity single stock traders were sitting in the middle of the floor constantly yelling at each other. I was at what was called the structured product desk, where we worked on convertible bonds and exotic options pricing. And that's where I first saw the disparity in pay between quants and traders.

If I worked in my job for six to seven years, I could have earned $300,000 to $400,000 per year. But in the front office there were third-year, junior traders making $500,000 in a relatively good year like 1999. That doesn't mean their lives were easy. I'm not exaggerating when I say that you needed to bring a sleeping bag to the office and that most guys used their apartments as a place only for a morning shower.

I was working hard too, getting to work at 7 a.m. and leaving after 7 p.m. and still being outlasted by my boss. I don't know how she kept up that intense level of work, but I soon discovered her secret. She often grabbed a bunch of Advil from the cabinet drawer and swallowed them with some water. In that environment, after a while coffee does not work anymore.

Goldman was a huge change for me. At my PhD program, I had worked two hours a day with complete flexibility over my time. Working on the trading floor at Goldman was like switching gears and accelerating from 30 miles an hour to 200. I constantly had multiple projects at hand, and my priorities sometimes changed daily. I started to make significant contributions right away in terms of pricing, hedging, and risk analysis.

At the end of my first year I got outstanding reviews, and I was promoted to a trader position at the structured product group. I remember attending summer associate training at the Mohonk Mountain House on the weekends during my second year. We stayed at a $500 per night hotel, and as I looked out over the autumn foliage blanketing New York State, I thought to myself that life was good. I was flying high and continuing the smooth, upward career arc I'd started in China.

CHAPTER 3

Entering the Jungle

I was excelling, working for one of the most revered companies on Wall Street, well ahead of my peers and looking at a comfortable career ahead of me. Working for Goldman straight out of school and being moved to the front-office trading floor is like winning the lottery on the first ticket you play. At least that's what it seems like to an outsider. Don't get me wrong—it was an awesome experience, and I learned a lot from the people there, but for someone like me there is always a new challenge to find and a brighter brass ring to chase.

I am an ambitious man, and when I came to the financial sector after graduate work, I wanted it all. I knew that my climb to the top could take years to achieve, but I didn't come into this life just to settle for mediocrity or a comfortable existence in the middle. I wanted the riches and the lifestyle of a Wall Street bigwig.

I soon realized that the reality of life at a sell-side environment (sell-side means that you work selling financial products or advice to clients) is that in the end you are beholden to other people—your coworkers and your clients—to build your fortune. I wasn't willing to wait for that; I knew that intellectually I was ready for a more challenging environment.

I was making decent money as a junior trader, but I knew that to really make it I would need to find a place where I could try out my own trading strategies. Even at that early stage of my career I knew that by giving up immediate gain I could earn more in the long run.

At that point in my career I wasn't using a headhunter to find work. I simply went online like everyone else and started looking for jobs at proprietary, or prop trading firms, where traders use their own strategies to trade the firm's money in exchange for a percentage of the profits. I wanted to see what life was like on the buy side.

Making the move from the sell side to prop trading wasn't an unusual movement on Wall Street. At Goldman, everyone has to be a small piece in a big machine, keeping it running smoothly and making money for the bank. On the buy side, however, you are free to find a strategy to make money for yourself, and your strategy belongs to you. It's much more like being a free agent in baseball or football: you can take your skills to the highest bidder.

After scanning through dozens of jobs online, I found an ad created by a trader named Todd. He worked for Mid Century Partners, a hedge fund run by a Wall Street legend known for his outsized income and equally outsized personality. Todd needed a quantitative analyst to help him develop trading strategies, and I needed a chance to try out some of my ideas. It was a match made in heaven...at least it seemed like it would be. I contacted Todd and sent him my resume.

As a trader at Mid Century, Todd was paid close to 20 percent of the profits he earned for the company, which was among the highest pay rates for any hedge fund. Most funds or prop trading groups paid their traders something like 10 percent of P&L, and Mid Century had consequently drawn some of the smartest traders on Wall Street through its front doors. Todd was who I wanted to be. He had worked at JP Morgan, had become a stand-alone trader, and was doing well for himself. If I wanted to play with the big boys, Mid Century was the place for me even though it had a reputation for being a volatile work environment.

I was nervous going to meet Todd for lunch. I was just twenty-six, and I wanted to make a good impression. I felt confident that I knew my stuff, but what would Todd think of me? Would he see me as a real asset and invite me into the world of prop trading?

Todd was a nice guy, and we hit it off right away. A few minutes into our meeting I was right at home with him, and after briefly discussing what he needed, I agreed to take the job as his developer with the agreement that eventually I would work my way up to trading. He said, "Let's get started as soon as possible; every second counts, and if I'm going to keep my winning streak up, I need to make things happen as soon as possible."

I have never seen a place with two more contrasting qualities. The atmosphere was so casual that people would show up in shorts and t-shirts when they wanted to. Many would work from home or come into the office for only three hours a day. But you couldn't let that fool you. Those people were successes and had come across strategies that made money. Their programs ran automatically, and they came to work only to keep up on new information or to research their next great idea. Underneath the casual fun was the most perilous atmosphere I have ever been a part of.

I remember telling him on my first day, "Todd, it will take a few months for me to get these ideas into a strategy. Is that still okay?" I'll never forget his response.

"That's fine, but the boss doesn't take shit from anyone, so we've gotta make this work."

Todd was right. It wasn't unusual to come in and see two or three new traders a week, replacements for the newly fired lot who had been kicked to the curb. People talked about someone else being fired like the weather or a Yankee's game, just part of everyday life.

Each trader worked on his own proprietary strategies with whomever he'd hired to help him. I worked directly for Todd and was on his payroll. He had a contract with Mid Century but paid me out of his take. He was essentially

Entering the Jungle

in competition with every other trader on the floor. If his returns weren't enough to impress the boss, he would get the boot and fast. That meant he was always in search of an edge, some new idea that would put him in the money. And he would guard any new idea with his life.

At Goldman, if you had questions you could talk to senior guys, and they would help you. It was very much a team environment in which everyone worked toward an overarching goal. At Mid Century, however, Todd and I were out there in the wind, battling the other traders to try to earn risk capital from the "pot" of money run by the company. Knowledge is power in a prop trading firm, and all the traders knew that the boss was always ranking us and would often fire the bottom three performers to make room for new talent. You don't want to teach other people even basic knowledge because it might end up putting them above you in the rankings.

I remember not realizing when I first joined the company just how protective people were. Todd was boasting one day about his million-dollar-a-year compensation and that he had made money at JP Morgan and Mid Century.

"What strategy do you run?" I asked him.

His face immediately turned red, and he said with a laugh, "If I tell you, I have to kill you." He was joking, but he was looking at me as though I were trying to pick his pocket. From then on I carefully avoided asking such questions.

In many ways, traders at Mid Century were equivalent to CIA agents living and working in an enemy country. Everyone around them was a possible foreign agent, and each day was a battle to keep from being found out. I remember walking past cubicles and hearing the voices stop until I'd moved further down the hall. When our group had meetings in conference rooms, we would listen for footsteps outside in case anyone might be listening in. There was so much secrecy that even the people in the cubicle next to you were never your friends or even friendly beyond a simple hello. And it wasn't just other traders.

I started to work on volatility forecasts right away. I built an *EGARCH (exponential general autoregressive conditional heteroskedastic) model to forecast single-stock volatility. It basically takes into account the fact that stock volatility tends to pick up when stocks prices drop, a well-known phenomenon.

Our goal was to try to forecast short-term stock volatility and to buy or sell options on certain stocks if the implied volatility was different from our forecast. I immersed myself with all the technical work, and soon we were able to start trading live.

The first time I almost got fired I had been at Mid Century for only two months. We put on my new options strategy to test it, and we were doing well on a small scale. We were betting on volatility, and at that level there was

Entering the Jungle

plenty of it. Vigilance is a requirement in any trading environment, though, and when Todd got a little lazy and didn't put on the right hedge for one option position. The market went against us one day, and he was called into the boss's office for a talking-to.

When you lost money for the boss, he could be an executioner, and one who kept his ax sharp. We had lost only a tiny amount of money compared to what we made in our main strategy, but when Todd left the boss's office, the verdict was clear: he didn't want Todd experimenting with new strategies for a while.

"What did he say?" I asked Todd when he got back to our desk.

"He said 'I don't want you to trade option strategies for now. You have to let Yi go.'"

I was floored, but Todd held his ground. When the boss called his desk to press the issue, Todd told him "If you want him fired, do it yourself." The boss didn't, and I continued scrambling for new ideas that might carry us through another month. This was a familiar scene at Mid Century: a trader and his staff fighting for their lives.

Desperation is the enemy of rational thought, and so Mid Century's managers had set up incentives to keep us from messing up. When you're desperate, you make random bets, so the bosses worked to keep that from happening. I never knew exactly what they were doing, but occasionally Todd got a call about a strategy we were trying and either pulled back from it or suggested we change our tack. It wasn't an uncommon game.

For example, if a trader was doing statistical arbitrage short-term trading and one day he mentioned to the boss, "I feel the opportunity is gone in my space and I want to try some long-term low sharp ratio strategy," that would raise red flag and get the boss's hand closer to the "launch" button.

My life at the time was bittersweet. I wasn't working a lot of hours at Mid Century compared to the weekends and late nights at Goldman. In fact, my first year at Mid Century was a sort of bittersweet ride. My wife, Xiaomin, was in Chicago working in her post-doctorate role at the University of Chicago, and so I was on my own, living as a sort of married bachelor. While I missed her, I was trying to enjoy my time alone living in a high-rise apartment and trying to fill my free time. I could never fully relax, though, because I never knew if I was going to have my job from one week to the next.

Eventually I developed a statistical arbitrage model. We were holding multiday positions in a basket of equity stocks, betting that the market would overreact and then come back. I worked from scratch, collecting the data for our strategy and doing the research. I was using C++ to create our program. Venturing outside our familiar territory took a lot of courage, since that would put us in direct competition with a lot of established strategists hired from outside the firm.

Entering the Jungle

It was like gold mining because we had to believe that our skills would lead us to a big payday. But the trouble was all worth it because it was the first time I could call myself a prop trader. I remember the joy and hopefulness of putting on a small position at the beginning. I guess it's the same feeling most start-up traders feel. The environment at this point in the process is very tough since the fund was an incubator for tons of strategies. Most of them did not survive. But it was the hopefulness that motivated people to work hard.

After a lot of ups and downs with our strategy, we gradually grew our position, and at the end of my time at Mid Century, we were trading a book of $200 million. In the end I decided to leave Mid Century because the compensation wasn't what I had hoped for and partly because we were running out of ideas. So after four years I called it quits.

Looking back, going to Mid Century was not a great decision for me financially. What was more detrimental, however, was that Mid Century was a barren desert when it came to on-the-job training or education. Everyone was so secretive about strategies that meetings were held before or after hours in locked conference rooms or off-site altogether. That meant that once you'd used up all of your own ideas, you were done. There was no one to share with or bounce ideas off; that would have been tantamount to giving away your bread and butter.

I had been a bright, cocky kid going into the experience.

Head of Research

I was confident in my abilities and convinced that going to a prop trading fund would buy me the golden ticket. And while I realized the prop trading model was ideal for me in a theoretical sense, the reality was so much harder than I had thought it would be. It really humbled me and brought me back down to earth.

It was my decision to leave Mid Century. Fortress was calling, and it was a bigger and more team-oriented environment. My wife was with me finally, having caved in to my requests that she move to New Jersey to be with me.

All of the firms at which I worked after Mid Century were buy-side firms because I still believed that those were the best places to be creative and to chase the big paycheck. After leaving Mid Century I was still looking for that big payday, and I thought Fortress would be the place to find it, so off I went.

CHAPTER 4

Life in a Fortress

After working at Mid Century for four years, I was eager to find new opportunities. Mid Century had challenged me but it had also shown me that proprietary trading was where I was happiest, and I wanted more of it. I almost felt suffocated at Mid Century and was desperate to find a firm that embraced the idea of teamwork. I had exhausted many of my own ideas at Mid Century, and I thought that a collaborative environment would help rekindle my creative juices.

In 2006 I started to interview with several prop trading groups, one of them being Fortress. I knew that Fortress would be more team oriented than Mid Century had been, and I hoped that I could play a larger role in one of their many groups. I wanted to work my way up the ranks of a place like Fortress because it would build my reputation and set me up for ever-more prestigious job opportunities.

My time at Mid Century hadn't earned me a sterling reputation in the financial world. Because Todd and I had done well but not remarkably well, I couldn't really lean on that experience to ask for a portfolio manager's role. I had been coy with most interviewers because I wanted to feel out what was available. My preliminary interviews with Fortress went well, and soon I was asked to do a last-round interview with Doug, the head of the Newton Group.

We were scheduled to have a breakfast meeting at the midtown Marriot Hotel, but Doug was fifteen minutes late, and I was getting impatient waiting for him. I paced back and forth, anxious to get the meeting started as formally dressed businessmen and women passed in and out of the lobby. That parade of dark suits and ties was soon broken by a middle-aged guy walking through the revolving door at the front of the hotel. He was unshaven, with wiry hair and frumpy clothes. He looked worse than my professors at Penn had looked, and he stood out like a sore thumb. Apparently so did I, because he walked toward me and said, "You look different than anyone here, so you must be Yi."

I stammered a hello, and we found a table in the restaurant. Doug ordered the smoked salmon with extra fruit on the side but only picked at his plate as we talked. As I ran through my resume and my ideas for Fortress, I wondered if I had his attention or if the fruit did. Then after a while he looked up and asked, "Do you have any questions for me?"

I wasn't sure what to say, so I asked something

Life in a Fortress

general. "Your group and this role has impressed me so far. I'm curious to know what your future plans are for the group?"

Doug didn't answer; he just started getting up and said, "Let me get back to your recruiter." I sat at the table for ten minutes after he left, thinking about how badly the interview had gone. I didn't expect to hear back from Doug.

Fortress wasn't offering me a lot of money, so I wasn't too disappointed in the meeting not producing a result right away. I began looking for other opportunities, but my confidence in myself overall was waning.

When I showed up on Wall Street I was a confident kid, a rising star with a PhD and a record of high performance. But it doesn't take long to lose momentum in the financial world, and I realized I had to act fast to take another step forward. I have never given up in my life, and my dream of Wall Street riches was still very much alive. So I waited to hear from Doug.

The phone rang at my home office, and when I picked up I was surprised to hear the head of human resources at Fortress. "Mr. Chen, we'd like to offer you a position with the Newton Group."

Doug had surprised me, but I was excited to get going. They were pretty vague about my bonus number since it was a new group and I wasn't entirely sure what I was going to be doing, but to me the opportunity to join a

Head of Research

strong collaborative team was worth some sacrifice. I just didn't realize how much sacrifice Doug had in mind. I realized my mistake quickly when on my first day at Fortress, Doug walked by and introduced me to other people at the company by asking them, "Did you meet our new developer?" My heart sank.

At Mid Century I had run a $200 million book under Todd's supervision. I was well beyond the role of developer, which is someone who constructs computer-managed trading programs. My heart broke a little bit when I realized Doug wasn't interviewing me for any form of trading or portfolio management. But I kept my head up and resolved to start from scratch in my new team. I surveyed the rest of the group around me, almost all of whom had quantitative PhDs, and I assessed my position.

In a prop trading team environment, it's crucial to identify the dynamics as quickly as possible because team dynamics are almost as important as performance, all other things being equal. If you want a chance to move up the ladder, you have to know who's in your path. Doug was the overall boss, and underneath him were Raj and Tom. While Raj would end up losing control of the group after that fateful week in August 2007, he was the most senior quantitative trader when I joined the group.

He had come from Goldman asset management, GSAM, and was a star in his own right. Raj was running a long-term currency book and a small macro equity book

Life in a Fortress

as well. Tom was covering high-frequency strategies that traded intraday global equity and currency futures. Tom had been the head quantitative analyst at the Royal Bank of Scotland (RBS) covering both derivatives pricing as well as prop trading. He had been a pretty big star there, and he was helping run the Newton group at Fortress.

Tom worked with Jeff, a managing director and head of IT who would be sitting beside me. He worked building the whole database and trading infrastructure using the R and C++ programming languages for both high-frequency as well as low-frequency strategies. Raj was interesting. As is the case with most successful people, he seemed confident, even arrogant at times. I didn't know him well when I walked through the door of Fortress in early 2006, but I learned that he is actually quite nice and hardworking.

After surveying the landscape in the Newton group, I quickly realized that I was the low man on the totem pole. I hadn't made big demands of Doug, and that made everyone think I wasn't worth respecting. I was teased when I first got there because I was an unknown quantity to the traders working with me. I wasn't about to sit around moping, though. I got right to work.

I was immediately put with Raj and started building the risk management system for the group's positions. At the same time I started working on several key strategies with him, and I soon proved my worth so much so that within a few months I became his only strategy support.

Raj was well respected at Newton, and by being attached to him I rose quickly in the ranks. While Tom was in charge of building our infrastructure, Raj raked in a huge P&L as head trader, and that created tension in the group. It didn't help that I was his go-to guy now and that my work was winning me praise from Doug.

Newton was a friendly group, but when you bypass coworkers, especially on Wall Street where everyone is competitive and ambitious, things are bound to get ugly. And they did in some ways. In addition to the teasing, there was a lot of talking behind my back at Newton during my first year. I could tell people resented my success and my rise through the ranks. But some of that resentment was blunted by the fact that we were doing really well. When everyone is making money, everyone is happy.

Despite the money, some people couldn't hide their feelings. Jeff was one of those people at first. He was nice enough, but our relationship became strained the more I invaded his areas of expertise. Jeff had worked with Doug at Goldman Sachs and was his golden boy in some ways. But with Raj's leadership I was asked to start looking into areas of our strategies that ended up getting me in trouble and further divided Jeff and me.

Our silent feud continued into 2007. In March 2007 we lost quite a bit of money by having bought too many positions and were thus overly long the market. We were actively considering using options to hedge the risk, and

Life in a Fortress

Jeff and I were assigned to work on this study. I was mostly just helping, but since options were part of my specialty, I did a quick backtest by going over the historial price data to check the hedging strategy.

I discovered that the strategy would gradually lose money, but occasionally we would see big gains in the event of a market crash. I sent my results to Jeff but I didn't want him to be the only person to see what I'd done. To be a little bit cautious since our relationship was a little tense, I sent my findings to Doug and Raj in the same e-mail. Doug looked at the graph and the gradual losses we would face, and he didn't like it. After flipping through the graph several times, he looked over at Jeff and said, "Can you check Yi's result?"

Jeff immediately hopped over to my computer. I explained my methodology, and he was immediately unhappy about a number of shortcuts I'd used. He looked back to Doug.

"There are some issues with Yi's results." Doug nodded his head, and this signaled Jeff to take over the work. He took my spreadsheet and spent the next two weeks fixing all of my dividends and rolling schedules and also cleaning up some of the raw data I had used. After two weeks of work he showed Doug a graph that was essentially identical to mine. Doug proudly told Raj, "See what Jeff did?" Raj just smiled; he knew that I'd done good work, but he had to let Doug have his victories.

It wasn't the only time I had my work co-opted by member of the team. Sitting next to me in the team was Con, a senior programmer who worked on high-frequency strategies with Tom. One day he threw up his hands in frustration and stared at his computer screen. He had been backtesting a new strategy, and things weren't working no matter what he tried.

"Hey Con, can I help?" I asked, thinking nothing of giving some of my time to a fellow trader.

"Yeah, Yi. I don't really know why this doesn't work."

I took a look at the data set and told him it might be better to rank stocks using different signals. I did a quiet study of the data in Excel and sent him my results and cc'd Tom. It was a mistake. Tom got this weird look on his face and looked over at Con as if to say, "What the hell are you doing getting Yi involved in high-frequency trading?"

It was the last time I worked on high-frequency trading at Newton, but I was soon vindicated. Con secretly told me that the group ended up adopting my idea and that it significantly stabilized their performance.

As 2007 rolled on, I was building up my workload and getting involved in more projects. Eventually I had proven myself on so many projects that Doug called Jeff into his office and had a long conversation with him. I don't know the details, but Jeff seemed to be a lot nicer to me afterward, and he even volunteered some support on later projects. But even seemingly positive steps in a tense

Life in a Fortress

trading environment have repercussions. Because Jeff started working with me more and more, Tom felt that his role was being threatened. In some ways he was right.

Doug created an environment in which jobs were fluid and official promotions were scarce. He didn't just announce someone had a new title; instead, he would simply ask one person to ease back on his responsibilities and ask someone else to fill them. Jeff was being asked to ease back.

Doug and Raj started discussing a promotion for me that would have meant bypassing Tom. When Tom heard about it, he started to become unstable. One day, while all the other team members were still at their desks in the early afternoon, he grabbed his bag and left. Doug was shocked; he immediately cancelled my promotion for fear of losing Tom. I was disappointed. I had learned during my years in the business to keep moving forward and to not let emotion take over.

I kept making progress, but every time Raj and Doug discussed my promotion, Tom resisted it. He was dead set against my promotion, and he carried enough weight in the group that eventually they decided against promoting me. It was a hectic time; it seemed like every other day I was either being promoted or being "un"promoted. Although frustrated, I just tried to do my job and not worry too much.

In July 2007, we started seeing real market volatility.

We had some pretty big swings in our currency book, so we started to look closely at macro strategy. Our currency models depended on long-standing factors that had held up well in the market since 2000. But eventually each of these factors started to break down as the markets panicked. There wasn't a real rhyme or reason to the markets we were in, and that challenged us.

What happened in the markets was like a snowball effect; when one or two multi-strategy funds start to unwind their positions due to sub-prime exposure, it drags down the performance of certain long-term strategies since most of the holdings are illiquid. Once that happens, it triggers a chain of events.

Eventually we landed on that August day, staring at our computer screens and wondering if the world was coming to an end. Oddly though, that week and those hectic, crazy moments allowed me to really shine. Doug saw that I kept my head and that in all aspects of the research, analysis, and improving the strategy I was not only competent but was also very capable. In the aftermath of our week off, I quickly became an important person in the group.

Taking credit and making sure others know what you've done is important on Wall Street. You have to say loud and clear what you've done, otherwise you can get lost in the shuffle. Although I made several significant contributions to the main strategy at Newton, I was somewhat overshadowed by Raj. He was the main portfolio manager and was also in charge of risk allocation of all strategies. Doug wanted to get me involved in that process a couple of times, but Raj wouldn't commit to the change.

Ultimately, Doug wanted me to take a more important role in the group, and that meant moving past Raj. He had been my mentor in many ways, and I had no interest in stepping on him. Eventually, though, the door would open for me to take over his role.

When it was time to do our annual performance reviews, I drafted a first version that stated my contributions and promised to work hard in the coming year as a senior portfolio manager. Doug called me into his office after reviewing it and said, "You need to do better than this."

I wasn't sure at first what he meant. He hadn't looked as serious for a long time, and he was making me nervous. The air conditioning in his office was running full speed, but I was sweating bullets. My time at Newton had been so volatile already that I had never gotten a good sense of my place in the group.

With Raj's support I had barely managed to get Tom and Jeff's collaboration in my projects. Now I was a senior portfolio manager running a sizable book, and I wanted to enjoy it for a moment, but Doug had such an urgency in his eyes.

So after thinking long and hard about my situation, I finally understood what Doug meant. He wanted me to take over Raj's role. I wanted to relax and get comfortable with my role, but our group was facing such a difficult situation that we needed new blood at the top.

Doug saw my potential to make better strategy decisions than Raj could and to save our group, so I rewrote my performance review. "Like the title character in the *John Doe* television series, always trying to find his true identity, I have tried to find out who I am here. And every project I worked on I discovered more about myself and what I can contribute to the team. I feel I am ready."

Doug called me into his office after having read my revisions. "Yi, it's time. Why don't you show us what you can do?"

I swelled with pride. I was now in charge of risk allocation and trading at Newton, but it also hurt. Raj had been my main supporter and defender, and now I was taking his position. It was my dream job, and I had so many ideas flowing through my mind that I was about to burst.

Unfortunately, so was the market.

We'd already shut down for a week that summer, but most of us thought the downturn was temporary, something we could work out of in time. We just had no idea how bad things were going to remain for the rest of the year.

I led the team through the end of 2007 and into 2008, but with less money to invest, we couldn't dig our way of the hole we'd fallen into in August. At the time my friends would talk about pre-2007 as a golden age of sorts when they could "make money without trying."

Being in charge of the group didn't mean that Tom would suddenly respect me or that Raj was happy to stay. We did what we could, but eventually the pressures of the market started to sour our interpersonal relationships. My personal performance was good, but like so many other groups at the time, we were simply caught up in the avalanche of failures.

As our positions grew more desperate, I could see the writing on the wall. I wanted to stay at Fortress and keep building something long-term, but eventually there was nowhere to go. Our group did not survive in the end, and in early 2008 we closed up shop, and I was once again on the lookout for a new opportunity.

CHAPTER 5

Taking a Step Back

It was a month after Newton had closed. I was out on the street again, looking for work and picking up the pieces of my career. You'd think at this point that I might give up and move on to a career that offered some form of stability. I learned, though, that I have huge reserves of persistence in me. I simply won't give up chasing my dream no matter how many times I get knocked down.

I don't mean I wasn't down or upset. I was. I had seen Fortress as a real chance to take my career to a new level in a team environment, and after Raj was moved aside and I took over, I did what I could to make that happen. Sometimes, though, you're just a passenger on the train and not the engineer.

As I sat in my home office reviewing job opportunities, one thing was abundantly clear to me. *This is going to be a tough one*, I told myself. The prop business at the beginning of 2008 was a minefield, and there was an added layer of risk to a business that never offered any guarantees in the first place. Most of the prop trading shops were still struggling with big losses, and at the time people were talking only to candidates with very high Sharpe ratios, like four or better.

The Sharpe ratio is a measure of how much reward an trader's strategies offer for every bit of risk. If you have a Sharpe ratio of four and can maintain it, you'll make yourself a mint on Wall Street. I didn't have a four at the time, and going into interviews felt like going into a sales meeting with no product to sell. And it wasn't just my Sharpe ratio.

Despite the fact that I had been running the group at the end of my time with Newton, 2008 saw a sizable shift in how people were trading the market. Because there was so much volatility, no one wanted to engage in low-frequency trading that might leave their assets exposed for too long to any one investment strategy. People just wouldn't bet on any one thing for too long because every day brought more bad news about the economy, and the market reacted to each news bomb.

High-frequency trading was suddenly taking over the show, which was a new place to be for the firms specializing in it. Most of the high-frequency trading firms operated behind the scenes prior to 2007 partly because people were making big money everywhere and didn't really need high-frequency setups to find a windfall.

Before 2007, most of the high-frequency traders were technologists. But because of the big sell-off in 2007 and the subsequent market volatility, it became a golden age

Taking a Step Back

for high-frequency trading. So I eventually decided to accept an offer from an equity quantitative research group at Bear Sterns in mid-February, thinking it might not be a bad thing to go high frequency. I had decided to postpone my start date for a few weeks and thus witnessed another episode in financial history.

I clearly remember my first day at Bear. It was March 17, 2008, the same day it was acquired by JP Morgan in an emergency buyout. On the first day of orientation, the place was in turmoil. Most of the new employees were sitting there, impatiently waiting for an HR person to show up and tell us what was happening.

Finally, a young kid came into the room we were waiting in. He couldn't have been more than twenty-four; he had boyish features and a suit that didn't quite fit. He was all smiles as he walked in the door, but I wasn't so sure. Before he came in to see us I saw him standing in the corridor, talking to his boss. He leaned in to talk with him and quietly asked, "Are we still good for orientation?" The boss nodded but mentioned that the kid should do something first. I couldn't make out what it was at first but found out as soon as he handed out our nicely prepared orientation booklets.

On the front he'd stapled two pages of the Bloomberg news article announcing the buyout with a statement from the head of Bear saying, "We are happy to be acquired by JP Morgan." Anybody who believed him was a fool.

Head of Research

Bear Stearns had a grand tradition, and here it was, being peddled off to another bank in an eleventh-hour sell-off.

I looked at the others in the room; I think we all realized that we were witnessing financial history. It was another hallmark in a series of hallmarks that saw even hallowed banks folding or being bought up for nothing more than their debt. That day was crazy; it was so odd to be sitting there during an orientation as the company essentially ceased to exist.

The HR kid stammered through his presentation, agitated and distracted. He lost his place several times and kept looking toward the door as though someone might come in to tell him that there was no need for his services anymore. He wasn't the only one. Although there was a nice breakfast and some good coffee at one end of the conference room, no one seemed interested. At every break people were taking out their cell phones to report the news to their friends and loved ones.

When I actually started work at the firm a day later, the Stern employees were still in shock partly because a lot of the stock they owned in the company was now worthless. It was painful to watch as Bear Stearns' stock price dropped from $150 to $50 in just over a year, eventually dwindling to just $2. These people were literally losing fortunes in front of their eyes. It just served as a reminder that nothing is guaranteed in this business.

After things settled a bit, I quickly got to work when I was assigned to do high-frequency market making for specialist firm Bear Wagner. It was an interesting project. The group was headed by Art Asriev, a Russian with gray hair. There was another Russian, Leonid, who was in charge of research and modeling. He moved with Art from ITG and had proven himself at Bear Sterns. All of the quants in that group reported to him directly on research issues.

The whole group was a nice mixture of Russian and Chinese people. Like most research environments it was somewhat laid back, and most of the production issues were handled by the IT department. Market-making strategy was a relatively new project for our group and the one on which Leonid started focusing exclusively after the acquisition. We worked closely together on that project.

My job initially was to implement the strategy in C++. Leonid had a thirty-page document of mathematical formulas and trading logic with over half a dozen market microstructure factors. It was like a blueprint for a car, and my job was to build the car.

We sat down to discuss the project one day, and I asked him the timeframe. He said, "Couple of months if you're good. Don't worry; Art and I will get more guys working on this later."

Three weeks later I knocked on his door and reported my progress. He was really impressed. After checking a few details, he was convinced that I was on the right track. He told Art that he didn't need more support on that strategy because I could handle it myself.

Art was in shock at first. He didn't believe that I could construct a significant portion of the strategy so quickly. But Leonid was his right-hand man, someone he trusted. Still, Leonid was used to working with a dozen quantitative researchers, and now he wanted to work only with me on the project. Although he was skeptical, Art let us continue.

Soon, after some more testing, we were ready to "go live" with the strategy. We test-traded a couple of stocks first. While testing, we made some noise in our group. Our strategy had us trading what would have amounted to 5 percent of the volume for stocks like Citigroup in one day. That got some senior manager's attention, including the CEO of Bear Wagner. Art wanted us to work this strategy to make a statement, but he certainly did not expect *that* kind of statement. He smoothed over the appropriate egos and made sure we were covered from too much further scrutiny.

After our strategy went live, Art started to quietly shift the group's weight toward me. I started to notice people paying more attention to me and what I was doing. Sometimes other developers in the group would come by to ask if I needed some help. The rumor was that I was going to receive a promotion, and I had a feeling that some of those people coming by were looking to latch on to a fast riser.

I couldn't help getting excited about the possibility

of a promotion. I was excelling at my work, and people were noticing, so it felt natural to be rewarded. But like all things on Wall Street, you have to hedge your bets and not assume anything. Just when I got pumped up about getting a promotion, the scene changed one day. There seemed to have been some discussion between Art and Leonid about me, and then no one mentioned the promotion any more.

I remember looking over toward Art's office one day to see Leonid coming out after a meeting, and he was looking uncertain. It wasn't long before I found out why a promotion would have been irrelevant. Rumors started spreading that JP Morgan was going to sell Bear Wagner.

Art's boss called me into his office several weeks later. I didn't know what the meeting was for, but I had a bad feeling about it. Talk of my promotion had gone quiet as the atmosphere in the market became more volatile. No one was sure what would happen to his job, and with so little time at the company I had no tenure. As I stepped into his office, I didn't think I was getting lucky. I was right.

"Yi, we're going through some transitions right now in the company." He paused and cleared his throat, "and your job has been…eliminated."

I nearly choked. I couldn't believe this was happening to me again. All I wanted at this point in my career was some stability. I just wanted to get past the depressing end to my time at Fortress, and I was doing well at JP Morgan. And then this.

"Yi, we will keep paying you until…" I couldn't hear him after that. My ears were full of sound, as though a freight train was running through my head. I just sat there, stunned, staring at his mouth moving as he tried to reassure me that my career hadn't just been turned on its head again. But what was I going to do now? I don't remember what he said after that.

There are only so many times the average person can start over, and I wasn't sure if I wanted to keep putting myself through the career wringer after my time at JP Morgan. I had to reassess what I wanted and if I had the personal fortitude to keep going, maybe at a lower-grade position than I wanted. There weren't too many fresh opportunities at this point, and each employee was clinging to any opportunity he could grasp. If I simply found a new job at all, I would have been thrilled.

I decided that I had to keep going. Quitting simply wasn't an option in my mind. I love the challenge of Wall Street, and if you want something as much as I did, you have to fight for it no matter how many setbacks you face. So I sent out my resume to headhunters and braced myself for another round of interviews that always seemed to get around to the duration of my jobs.

"Tell me, Yi, why is it that you've been at so many employers in the last couple of years?" they would all ask.

I didn't have an easy answer to give them; I told them the truth, about the economic volatility and the challenges of establishing myself as the head guy. Some seemed satisfied with my explanations, but I could tell others saw me as tainted goods.

CHAPTER 6

Climbing the Turret, Part I

After leaving JP Morgan, I wasn't sure where the next opportunity for me would come from. I had handled a lot of responsibility and had had the potential for high earnings at Fortress, and I wanted that for myself again. In early 2009, after searching out the best possible situation for my family, I got lucky and was hired as a high-frequency portfolio manager at Turret Capital, which specializes in quantitative trading and investment strategies. I was hired by the CEO of the company, Phillip Smith, who offered me the chance to earn a sizable income. And I felt I needed it; my wife was pregnant with our first child.

As a portfolio manager I would have a significant P&L associated with my contributions to the company. And since I had worked as a quantitative analyst just prior to this job, it was a big step up for me. Phillip, a very smart guy, is a billionaire and a successful entrepreneur to boot. He welcomed me to the company with some very kind words, telling me, "I don't know if you have a good trading strategy or not, but we all liked you. I think you're smart, and I'll give you twelve months to prove yourself." It felt like a new beginning for me.

Phillip's generosity was in keeping with the atmosphere he'd created at his company. The environment in the office was cordial, familial, and comfortable. The office itself was full of large, lush plants—a veritable rain forest in the middle of New York City. I'd never been in an office before where people took turns cooking for each other on Fridays and where strollers were a normal sight on the floor. It was encouraging, but I couldn't take time to enjoy the ambiance. As I'd learned so many times before, you can't take your position for granted on Wall Street.

I worked hard from the beginning, coming in early and staying late. I knew that the clock was ticking for me, and so I poured myself into the C++ and Matlab coding I needed to create my strategy. I didn't want to get distracted by the jovial atmosphere, and so I put my head down and worked hard during the week and almost every weekend. My small office was adjacent to the larger office where the managers sat.

In May, my first child was born, a girl, and I was thrilled. I took a week off from work to be with my wife and daughter and to really enjoy the moment. I was lucky to have my parents-in-law in town to help take care of a lot of the babysitting and housework. Phillip congratulated me on the occasion, and it seemed that things were going to work out at Turret for me. I was working very hard, and Phillip took well to that, even suggesting to the other employees that if they worked as hard as I did we would be even better off as a company.

I continued to push, working late and then heading home to help change diapers and do bottle feedings with my daughter. I couldn't help think about strategy, though. At 2 a.m. I would be standing over the changing table in my daughter's room, changing her diaper, and realize that I was running through coding problems or my strategies. And then I would turn around and be back at the office before 8 a.m.

But my life was fulfilled, and I really enjoyed what I was doing. As a young trader I wanted to work hard to pay Phillip back for his trust.

It's amazing how quickly things can go bad when everyone is under a lot of pressure. My mistake was a simple one, but it would pit me against a powerful figure within the organization and cause friction at the very highest levels of management. It all began innocently enough.

Turret hired a lot of undergrads as developers, but over time they encouraged these guys to move out of the development role and into the trading teams as prospective traders or quantitative analysts. And there was a great deal of incentive for these developers to make this move. The pure developers aren't paid very much and are therefore eager to join a successful trading group.

When one of these programmers, a young guy named Tim, approached me one day, I thought nothing of it. At that time he was still working in the IT department on a relatively big project. He offered to work for me in his spare time on an informal basis, doing some development work. At the time I wasn't sure if I could hire someone on my budget, but I knew that having the extra help would allow me to start trading sooner.

I agreed to allow Tim to help on the technical side of my project. I was swamped with coding tasks as I tried to implement my trading strategy. We agreed, however, that because I wasn't a proven quantity Tim wouldn't mention his involvement with my project until we were sure he was a good fit and that his work with me was okay.

Tim worked for me for two weeks until Roger, his boss and the chief technology officer found out. He was furious. As a member of IT, Tim had access to data about each trader's performance and strategy. It was information that most of the traders didn't have access to since each strategy was considered proprietary. Roger believed Tim was being used by me to gain valuable information about the other traders and their strategies.

When I had brought Tim onto my team, I had no idea just how damaging it would be to my reputation at Turret. Roger was a powerful man in the company and in effect ran the day-to-day operations since Phillip was more of a hands-off, laid-back leader. Roger had spent two years

Climbing the Turret, Part I

building the whole infrastructure-risk analysis system for the firm. Phillip trusted Roger to make a lot of decisions for the firm, including hiring and firing, and I had just pissed Roger off.

Roger was worried that Tim would set a bad example for the others, that his move would encourage the IT talent to look elsewhere for work, and that the traders would look bad for stealing each other's codes. He was made more paranoid by two famous lawsuits at the time involving Goldman Sachs and Citadel that involved code theft.

Tim was fired, though he had done nothing wrong in my eyes, and Roger soon turned his disapproval toward me. For a while I looked really bad. Here I was, a new trader, not even trading for the company yet, and I had the second-most powerful person in the company virtually accusing me of internal espionage. Each day we were all summoned before Roger for a meeting on information security, and it wasn't any secret who in the room was the target of these talks.

It was a really tough time for me because I hadn't started trading yet and I had no positive record with the company to stand on. The other traders looked down on me as a cheater, someone out to steal their secrets. I couldn't believe it was happening to me, but I wasn't about to give up and walk away from a great opportunity at a good company. I did the only thing I could. I showed up to work and pushed myself to get my programming completed, even as random traders stopped by the other desks and pointed my way, snickering about how there was a snake in the room. Even the technology guys, the same people who had been eager to hitch themselves to my wagon at the beginning of my tenure, stayed away from helping me.

The environment was openly hostile toward me, and I was heckled often, even by young programmers who would yell, "Get the bad apple out of the door." But nothing bothered me. I just worked like a machine and tried my best to repair the relationship with Roger. I tried to explain to him what had happened and how innocent my mistake was, but he was intractable.

One day I overheard Roger on the phone with Phillip. He said "What do you think of him? Why don't we let him go?" Luckily for me, Phillip resisted those notions since I had been onboard for only seven months. But Roger was insistent and kept pushing Phillip to listen to him and to fire me. Eventually Phillip must have drawn a line in the sand, because Roger slammed the phone down and rushed out of his office, looking at me with murderous rage on the way out.

All I could do was work hard with my strategy. I told myself, *I cannot control these people; I am not going to let these things bother me, ever.*

For next few days Roger avoided work and might have

Climbing the Turret, Part I

even threatened to leave the company if Phillip didn't get rid of me. I think their battle was about more than me and my mistake. It was a clash of wills and a test of who really wielded control in the company. Roger felt undervalued by Phillip, and so he was testing his position by being absent. He was out for two days in a row, and Phillip grew more stressed by the hour.

Phillip had a tough decision to make. He could fire me, a new member of the team, and keep his CTO happy, or he could stick to his guns and back me up based on the potential he saw in me. Phillip, though, wasn't fully equipped for life without Roger, and Roger knew that. Phillip had trouble even getting someone to fix a computer glitch he had while Roger was out, and I could see my chances of survival begin to slip away.

One day Phillip stayed late, almost past 7 p.m., in a meeting with our chief operating officer John. They were discussing something, though I didn't know what. Next to Phillip was Roger's empty seat. All of the traders had left for the day already, and the office was so quiet I could almost hear a pin drop.

I overheard John say something about the "paperwork" and how it was already "on the table." I was still working hard, and alone, on my project just as I always had, but I couldn't help listen to them talking. I heard Phillip on the phone with Roger trying to persuade him to give me another chance. I knew that John was there for one reason: to pull the trigger if Phillip lost his battle with Roger.

But Phillip couldn't do it. He couldn't let me go, and instead of giving John the go-ahead, he told Roger "I can't do it." The next day he told me that I had the green light to start trading. I was in shock. I had been seconds away from being fired for a simple mistake; I had been labeled a cheat and had been blackballed by the technology workers, and yet here I was with the full support of the CEO.

CHAPTER 7

Climbing the Turret, Part II

After nearly losing my job after being there for just seven months, I decided to throw myself into my work. I never gave up hope that my strategy would work or that I could win over the people I worked with if my performance was good enough.

A couple of weeks after Phillip saved me, I finished testing my strategy setup. The eight months it had taken me to complete my strategy were the hardest months of working in my life. Because of my run-in with Roger, I was working alone, essentially constructing a trading program from scratch. After all of that work I was ready to begin trading, and I crossed my fingers before going live. I needed it to work.

Trading started off with a bang, returning a positive trading P&L. I was ecstatic. All of my work looked like it would pay off. My strategy centered around providing liquidity by capturing rebates. My average P&L was 0.4 to 0.5 cents per share, beating the rebate of 0.3 cents per share, and for a few days in a row the results were astronomical. I could hardly believe it, and I wasn't the only one who was incredulous.

Phillip was paying close attention to my progress, and after another great day of trading he actually asked the chief operating officer, "Is this P&L real?" He simply couldn't believe that my program was so successful, and he was thrilled because it vindicated him in his battle with Roger. I had been branded a cheat, but here I was proving my own strategy in the face of overwhelming doubt.

Late in the afternoon that day, he put his earphones on and bobbed his head to the music. He stayed that way for more than half an hour. I had never seen him so happy. On his way out of the office he walked by my desk, and I looked up and met his gaze. His look was something I'll never forget: a mixture of pride and approval that made me feel so glad that I hadn't disappointed him.

My success was surprising to everyone. In 2007 and 2008, high-frequency traders were in heaven because the market swung wildly up and down in a single day. We witnessed some financial stocks move 30 to 50 percent intraday. That kind of huge swing created plenty of opportunity for high-frequency trading firms and made a lot of money for a lot of people, which naturally attracted competition. By 2009, most of the market making strategies had a profit margin of 0.1 to 0.3 cent per share. My profits were double what the average market-making strategy was earning and that was encouraging.

Climbing the Turret, Part II

I must not have been the only one so encouraged by the news because a rumor soon started making its way across the trading floor: I was being considered for the head of research, a role that Phillip had been contemplating for the company but that didn't exist at that time. It would involve heading the research for new strategies. I have plenty of background in various quantitative trading areas, and he believed that quantitative trading might be the next step for high-frequency trading. At a prop trading firm this was really, really big news and not at all welcomed by the traders.

Their unhappiness had to do with one thing and one thing only: money. High-frequency traders generally get a pretty good payout for their strategies, sometimes hauling in 50 percent of the P&L since they were essentially creating and running the strategies for the company. At Turret, some senior traders were paid well over $1 million a year, but that pay relied on the fact that they had a proprietary trading strategy that was their own. It wasn't common knowledge how each trader earned money for the firm, and as long as it stayed that way, each trader had something valuable to offer.

As head of research I would have been surveying each trader's strategy to look for areas where research could be made more efficient for the firm. After all, it wasn't uncommon in some places for traders to be walking the same paths looking for returns, and it wasted a lot of time and valuable resources. But for each trader, having a head of research snooping through their strategies was akin to handing over their checkbooks.

The head of research role was something many firms had flirted with creating, but there was so much resistance from traders that few had done it. A further complication was that any head of research would know so much about a firm's strategies that he or she would be invaluable and could never be fired without some guarantee that that head wouldn't just go out and sell the information to the highest bidder.

Whoever won the head of research role would also be making a great deal of money, millions per year based on a percentage of the overall profits and losses. It was a coveted but perilous role.

When the news got out that I was being considered for it, I broke down and cried at my desk. Two weeks beforehand I had been fighting for my survival, saved only by Phillip's belief in me. It had kept me going during the toughest stretch of my career, and I was glad that I could pay back Phillip's trust. I felt like my hard work in the prop trading world was finally paying off. I was about to make a big step up in my career.

My joy was in sharp contrast to the deep anger of the management team and among the traders, and it was directed at me. Some traders were so upset at the idea of me seeing their strategies that they mockingly handed

Climbing the Turret, Part II

over their private banking information, insinuating that I could more easily rob them that way without ever seeing their strategies.

John's phone was ringing off the hook, and he kept explaining to various trading groups about Phillip's plan, trying to calm them down. Although he was very upset himself, since unlike Roger's role as CTO, the head of research role would be directly over his, and I would become his boss. Because of the complicated relationships within the firm, the rumors about my promotion changed daily.

One day, facing a lot resistance, Phillip decided that they were not ready to offer me the promotion. News got out in the afternoon, and everyone was happy and congratulating each other. One senior trader said, "Gosh, when we see Yi's face tomorrow it's going to be a Kodak moment."

For me the change of heart meant I would go back to being a nobody, a new trader with no clout in the firm. I would have no way of defending myself against Roger. I tried very hard to compose myself and finish my work. I don't know how I got home that night. I was devastated at the news. I had come so close to getting my dream job, and here I was being cast aside.

At home, my wife was busy taking care of our baby. When I got home she had just finished feeding her and was holding her close to her chest. Those two were so close to each other I wanted to cry. I just couldn't tell her the news and ruin that moment.

I tried very hard to keep my work drama to myself. I don't know how I got to bed that night without breaking down, but I didn't want to disappoint my wife. I lay in bed, overwhelmed with sadness and disappointment. I tried to find a way to make it all more manageable, and I thought about how just a few weeks prior I had almost gotten fired by Roger and how at least I was still a trader with a successful strategy.

The next day, I got in even earlier than normal. I met a couple of system guys on my way into the company, and they looked like they'd seen a ghost. Immediately they started asking each other if the boss's decision was real, because it if had been, a normal trader would have left the company immediately. Wall Street is built on reputation and respect, and when you're up for a big-money position you can't ever go backward. But here I was, assuming my old role.

When Phillip stepped into the office a little bit later, the surprise on his face was obvious. He quietly snuck past me to his seat as if he was not sure of himself or didn't want to disturb me. I heard him said to the chief operating officer, "This is amazing."

I tried to act normal, and for the whole day the other traders gawked at me as if I were a circus attraction. People were absolutely shocked to see me doing normal things like grabbing breakfast or taking a cup of tea. Everyone had been so pissed or so sad days earlier, depending on where the rumor mill was in its cycle, and yet I had managed to live through it.

I sat in my chair, watching trades flow through my monitor. I felt heavy, as though my weight would push on the chair so hard it would break. I almost stood up to leave, but I was having a good trading day, and I simply couldn't quit. I tried to calm down, but the people close by wouldn't let me. They were crying, moved by all of the drama and my resolve in the face of public failure.

I was so sad that I wanted to give up and leave, but then I felt the strength well up from inside of me. I was burning inside, shining almost. This was my ultimate belief in myself, and it was such a wonderful feeling that I didn't fear anything anymore. I kept telling myself, *I'm still a trader; I can still make a million dollars myself the hard way.*

The only time I got a little bit emotional was that afternoon when I heard Phillip take a call from Doug, my former boss at Fortress. I knew that Turret had done a thorough background check before they considered me for the head of research role, and Doug had pulled for me. Phillip tried to explain the roller-coaster ride to Doug.

"We know he is smart enough for this role, and thanks for the recommendation, but we are not ready to make this move yet."

I couldn't hear what Doug was saying, but he must have kept pushing.

Phillip replied after a long pause, "Sorry. We really tried."

My heart sank, but it also filled with warmth. Doug had really fought for me. It was surprising because Doug was an interesting guy, not prone to openly showing support or affection. In fact, after I left Fortress we lost touch. So his absolute support was very much a surprise to me in my desperate situation. I burst into tears and rushed to the bathroom to be alone. I was so overwhelmed with emotion. I composed myself and returned to work.

Maybe it was a mixture of several factors, but in the afternoon the playing field had changed again, and Phillip was considering reversing his position. Phillip sat down with me the next day. I was eager to hear what he had to say. He started with my strategy. "You did well so far, but I think you need some tech support to ramp up the trading. Right now we have another guy doing low-latency market-making strategy. He worked with his own programmer, and we decided to help him try out technology improvement first."

He was avoiding any talk of the head of research role, but he was clearly looking for a way to move me up the ladder. He added "What else can you do? You cannot do risk, programming, or compliance."

"Why don't we look at a way to bring the research

efforts of the groups together?" I said, still pushing for the idea.

He said, "Do you think that would work? Why don't you talk to several guys to start with?"

I started to talk to several traders in the company, but it was quite clear that that tactic wasn't going to work. The traders were too emotional because they feared losing control over their strategies. Some of them couldn't even talk to me calmly. The managers were also pissed, and they brought their objections to Phillip himself. Phillip was a nice guy, but he realized it would be too difficult to establish the role.

Phillip treated everyone like his own family, and he realized he was not going anywhere without the majority of the traders' support, especially because he would have to pay me a lot. After I failed to gather support, he told me, "I am not a dictator." I realized he was fighting a losing battle. I knew he liked me, but I also felt his struggle deep in my heart as well.

After a back-and-forth a couple more times, it wasn't long before Roger got his way. He sat me down in the conference room and fired me. I was so calm when he announced the news that it put him off guard. He lost his composure a few times and yelled at me for the "mess" I'd created. He had barely retained his role in the skirmish with Phillip, and he blamed me.

I can still remember overhearing the conversation

between Phillip and Roger at the end of their battle. Roger asked him, "What did Yi miss? A million-dollar role?" Phillip said, "At least two." I could hear Roger laughing at me, loud and crude. I felt extreme sadness and emptiness.

I walked back to my seat and said my good-byes to my fellow coworkers. They were all crying, and so was I. This was the first time in my career that I'd been considered for a seven-figure role, and the emotions it stirred in me made me realize just how much I'd sacrificed to get the opportunity.

I somehow made it home and walked through the door to see my little baby with my wife, who was still working to help support us. I was so close to collecting that big paycheck, and I wanted it so badly so that she could stay at home to take care of our baby full time. Instead, she was now the only one supporting us; I was once again unemployed.

I was a little bit numbed the first few days afterward. I remember one day after my parents and my wife had all gone to bed. I was browsing the Web like a robot. It was very quiet and dark outside, and all of a sudden I started crying. I couldn't stop. Then I heard my mom wake up and begin crying. It was the saddest moment in my life. She had not only given birth to me, but she had always given me all her support and hope. She had made huge sacrifices to let me come to the United States to pursue my dream, and my dream had been shattered.

Climbing the Turret, Part II

After some time I calmed down a little bit. I started to reflect on the volatility of my early career with Mid Century and Fortress. Those experiences cultivated my character and made me realize my own potential and will. At Turret, experiencing the huge embarrassment of being treated like a dog and the ups and downs of almost getting fired while being considered for a million-dollar role gave me an inner strength I had never known before.

The only way to keep myself balanced was to insist that my evaluation of myself didn't depend on what other people thought of me. Had I had any doubts about myself, I would have surrendered a long time ago.

Although I did not get that million-dollar role in the end, I discovered a different side of myself. This made me more motivated, more hungry, more eager to challenge myself. I established a new goal: a mid-level role in an established team environment. My will to survive pushed me forward once again.

CHAPTER 8

The Imperial Bank, Part I

If I've learned anything from my experience on Wall Street, it's that persistence is key to getting what you want in life. So many people give up on something if it's too hard or if they hit a few snags in their plan. By the time I left Turret I'd hit more than a few snags, but I was still as determined as ever to find a good job for myself. I began contacting recruiters and interviewing for different positions. I was like nothing they'd ever seen.

Recruiters look for people with stable job histories. They want to be able to point at your resume and tell an employer, "See? He's valued by employers, and he's loyal." My sporadic job history was always a topic of conversation as were my choices for job title. Usually, conversations with recruiters started like this:

"What asset class are you looking for?"

"Cash equity, but I can also do global macro and derivatives."

This answer was often followed by a period of silence because my range of experience wasn't as specific as they liked to hear. They would follow up with something like, "What senior level are you looking for?"

"I am open to from head of research down to quant developer. Frankly, I don't really care, since the jumps from junior quant to senior quant to trader are only a few projects away from each other in my experience."

There was usually a longer silence as the recruiter processed the idea that someone who had held senior positions would be open to the idea of "backsliding." My answer to this question would always lead to the real elephant in the room. "Why do you switch so many jobs?"

I would point at my resume and explain as best I could what happened at each post. "I lost the job here as the head of my group, and here and here as head of research. I don't know what's wrong, but maybe I got promoted so fast that I either had to take over or get out."

That answer would get most recruiters' heads spinning, since they always wanted to squeeze me into some specific role or range. They want to go to employers and say "Here is Yi Chen, your next senior vice president, quantitative analyst," or whatever the job opening happens to be. Selling a jack-of-all-trades is hard when most people stick to an onward and upward approach and leave the business if their career trajectory gets stalled.

Eventually I got two offers, one at a small trading firm that offered a high payout but also high risk, and the other as a vice president, quantitative analyst at a famous prop trading group at Imperial Bank. This group was the "crown jewel" of the investment bank. Eventually I decided to take the Imperial Bank offer, hoping for some stability. Unfortunately, that stability never came. Once more my experience would look tempting to my soon-to-be bosses, and once more it would cause friction with the people around me.

The head of the group was William, a short, middle-aged man, but my direct boss was Shaun, who had recently come from another famous trading shop. Like any typical, successful trader, he was pretty smart, but he also knew how to manage and manipulate people. Sometimes he bought you coffee or beer, and other times he jumped down your throat if you screwed up. He doled out encouragement and rebuke in equal measures depending on what he needed from you.

Our group had close to a hundred people who occupied a big trading floor. We had traders covering a diversified asset class, and the group overall had done really well in the past, even in very tough years like 2007 and 2008. Today it generates almost $1 billion in profits a year. And since traders generally get paid by their contribution to those profits, I estimated that at the time of my employment, traders there were sharing a $100 million pot every year. That's why we are called the "crown jewel" of the bank.

Donald Trump used to describe business life as being

tougher than survival in a jungle. I could not agree more. The front-office prop trading environment was like an urban war zone; people were constantly fighting for projects and ownership of profits. In a team environment, people fought to get other resources such as programming help. Since everyone always had multiple projects on hand, trying to get the programmers' attention to work for you was key.

Excelling at Imperial Bank meant that each of us had to act as Special Forces troops in an urban war zone, acting quickly and without mercy. It was pretty telling to see how a senior trader established himself or herself within the new group. Shaun was relatively new to the group. He had joined in April, a few weeks before I had. Shaun did a pretty impressive job when he first came in, making friends with traders of similar seniority while sometimes pushing hard on junior ones.

The most junior trader in the index arbitrage group, where I worked, was a guy we called B-Money. B-Money looked like a jock; he was well built and tanned and had a rebellious streak that sometimes got him in trouble. He shared an area with Shaun, a trader named Max, and me. One day, B-Money showed some unwillingness to do one tedious spreadsheet task for Shaun. It escalated quickly, and he was called into William's office for a talk. That taught everyone else in the group a lesson as well.

Our little group was focused on Exchange Traded

The Imperial Bank, Part I

Funds (ETF) strategy, but we were under the umbrella of a larger index arbitrage group. Shaun sat directly behind me along with Max. When I first got to Imperial Bank I was looking only to fit in and get along. I just wanted to do my work in a team environment. But anonymity just wasn't in the cards.

My first assignment was to work on strategy improvement and development for our group, which it turned out was a breeding ground for many of the firm's senior managers. I immediately felt like I was under a microscope, being carefully examined by the senior traders sitting around us. It was uncomfortable, but I did my best to keep my head down and my work consistent. It wasn't long, though, before my background became a topic of conversation in the office.

I made the mistake of mentioning that I had been a senior portfolio manager at Fortress and on track to be head of research at Turret. People couldn't believe that I was promoted that fast in a few different fields, and soon I was suspected of lying about it. One day, I heard B-Money talking to the trader next to him, saying, "If he's that senior, why would he even come here instead of retiring?" He didn't realize how much I wished I had been able to retire on a stack of money. It was hard to explain my journey to people who were used to seeing people either rise to the top or flame out and leave and not stick with it, as I had.

Head of Research

B-Money's attitude changed quickly one day when the big IT boss walked by another programmer and said, "That was pretty impressive. Everything on his resume checked out." All of a sudden I had some cachet to my name, and Shaun started to get me involved again on various projects. I was focused on an international ETF project at first because we knew that ETFs were becoming a popular trading tool since people wanted to buy diversified investments.

International ETFs were a big opportunity for a group like ours. They use a basket of underlyers, that is, the actual stocks that were underlying the ETFs, that are traded globally and do a lot of intraday volume. The challenge was that most often the underlyers in the ETFs don't trade at the same time as the ETFs themselves. For example, FXI has a basket of twenty-five Hong Kong stocks that trade from 9 p.m. to 3 a.m. U.S. time. So in general the opening price of FXI at 9:30 depends on the closing price of the basket at 3 a.m. as well as the futures movement from 3 a.m. to 9:30 a.m. Our plan was to create a market by creating a fair-value model for international ETFs in U.S. trading hours. I quickly jumped into the work, hoping to get ahead of other established firms in this business.

By this point in my career I was so diversified that results came quickly to me. I was proving my worth yet again, and soon the senior managers started to reevaluate my position. When I first got word that change might be in

The Imperial Bank, Part I

my future, I was both excited and skeptical. I didn't want a senior position without a lot of support because I'd seen at Turret that being made senior in the wrong circumstances can mean the end of your time at the company.

And yet I couldn't help but dream of the corner office...

For years had been envisioning myself in a big leather chair in a grand corner office with a sweeping view over Manhattan, watching various stats fly across my big-screen monitor. Senior traders would come to my office in turn and update me with all the results and issues of the day.

I also dreamed of moving to a mansion in New Jersey, where a lot of the Wall Street bigwigs have homes. I dreamed of expensive meals at fancy restaurants and appearances on *MSNBC*. And all of a sudden, after my miserable experience at Turret, I finally felt like I was on track to live that dream.

While I was dreaming, however, my coworkers were in revolt.

When the idea of my being promoted first came out, it triggered a bomb on the trading floor. I certainly couldn't believe the news myself, but the traders were downright irate when William, the head of the group, walked by my desk and said "I might as well sign him up for the management committee."

The traders at Imperial Bank had the same concerns as

Head of Research

had the traders at Turret: that their ideas would be stolen and that they would lose money or become redundant. Most of the senior traders got paid by their P&L contributions, so once I peered into their moneymaking secrets, they feared they would become dispensable.

Sitting in the next aisle from me was a group of fundamental traders. Unlike quantitative traders, they are a more-talkative bunch and even funny sometimes. One day, one of the guys in that group who focused on politics and macro news was on the phone, complaining about me. He said, "I am just a prop trader at a bank, what can I do to stop his promotion?" Another guy said, "We should start talking to him about our compensation." The mood of the room turned quickly against me. People were losing control everywhere. For a while everyone retired to the bathroom to cry or to complain to friends on the phone. The stresses of a job in the field can be demanding under any circumstances, but when you think all of the rewards for your hard work are going to be taken away, it can be too much.

I had joined Imperial Bank in a research role, and jumping up to head of research would have been huge. I had yet to make a real contribution, though, and that made those directly above me take notice. My group had over a dozen managing directors, followed by directors and then vice presidents like me. Despite the name, the "head of research" basically oversees all strategy, and for

The Imperial Bank, Part I

prop trading businesses, that means knowing everything about how they make money.

Our group was generating $1 billion a year, and once you know the secrets to making $1 billion a year, you cannot be fired. It is an extremely senior role, but on the other hand one that is almost immune to office politics, because a man with those secrets is too important to let go. The job would have meant $1 million to start with, and more to come later.

I was anxious. I didn't want to assume anything, but there was so little information coming out of senior management that I was completely in the dark. All we heard were rumors, and that was toxic to the working environment. I kept working on my regular assignment nonetheless and tried not to get too distracted.

Soon I heard about a meeting between William, the head of IT, and the head of trading one night. I don't know what they discussed, but I assumed it was about the new management arrangement and how I could fit in.

The next morning the head trader, who sat near to me, saw the unemployment numbers coming out on Bloomberg. He received a text on his phone and then turned and smiled at me while yelling out "unemployment!" I knew I was in trouble.

It wasn't the first time I had gone through something like this, so I kept my head and worked on my project. I thought I was a goner, but that afternoon I was saved by William. He began calling each trader into his office, I assume to lay down the law. He told them that he was considering me for the role, and from the impression I got from the traders, he had told them to mind what they said about it.

I could tell from the looks on the traders' faces after each meeting that they were unhappy. This dissention got me thinking about my chances should I step up now, and I decided to pass on the opportunity. For many people that would have been a crazy decision, but I was too experienced to walk into a job without official, open support from the senior managers.

On top of that, I had yet to make any significant contribution. Trying to take over a bunch of senior traders two levels above me would have been nothing but suicidal. On top of that, William had offered me the role only through indirect means, essentially by telling others I was charge. He had yet to announce anything publicly or to discuss options with me in person.

At one point, Kaz, a young trader with a sailor's penchant for swearing, started to mimic what I might sound like in the role of head of research. He joked with B-Money that I would say, "I am the *gatekeeper!* Let me make the decisions for you." The other guys were laughing too, but what they didn't realize was that I might as well have been called the "doorman." I wasn't getting paid for any new responsibilities, but I was catching all the flack of being a boss and then some.

The Imperial Bank, Part I

My feelings at this time were really complicated. Although I wanted the million-dollar role badly, I knew that I couldn't survive it as I though it was being offered. After all, I was a VP, and head of research was three levels ahead of me. And to be honest, from my past experience, I knew there would be other opportunities for advancement down the road that wouldn't cause so many problems. By essentially refusing to assume the role, I was telling William "No thank you."

My refusal, in the form of inaction, had a dual effect. It surprised William, and it endeared me to the traders who saw a different side of my personality. I wasn't chasing the brass ring as quickly as they might have, and that just plain confused them.

Some of the traders started to talk about my cool demeanor in a pressure-cooker situation, saying, "That's why he is so good; he can make impossible decisions that we can't. Only he knows it's a trap." Some of the traders even started to like me and admired my ability to make quick market decisions under pressure.

But I had no idea how much pressure was just about to come my way. William was gearing up a major push in favor of my promotion, and the trading floor was about to explode.

CHAPTER 9

The Imperial Bank, Part II

By having rejected the informal offering from William, I was slowly changing people's opinions about me. I started to have strange meetings without my direct bosses and with the heads of other departments, such as IT. In the business world, the hierarchy is very important, and since Shaun directly oversaw my ETF strategy, any meeting without him was unusual.

Shaun also organized some group meetings to gather the index arbitrage team together. I assumed that this was part of the plan to establish me as a leader, but I must have been wrong because when I opened a discussion about new research ideas, the other team members offered nothing and refused to participate.

Despite these snags in our meetings, I continued to focus on my ETF strategy. People started to say "He's not interested in head of research unless he gets paid and it happens to work out." William sometimes approached Shaun and said cryptic things that confused me, like "do you have $25 million?" Shaun wasn't about to explain what that meant to me. My relationship with him was strained.

As the summer approached, the situation began to deteriorate. Friday afternoons especially were tough for me because William usually left early for his big mansion in New Jersey. One Friday, as he was headed out the door, he told everyone except me, "I'm out of here; if you have any problems, report to Yi." I was sitting in the index arbitrage row, the center of the trading floor, and directly in front me were the statistical arbitrage group and fundamental traders who had raked in over $300 million the year before. A few rows behind me were senior high-yield bond traders and mortgage traders who had also been successful. They had made close to $500 million and were sitting on a multi-billion dollar book. They were not only elite traders, but they were also angry and frustrated because of the boss's decision.

The traders unleashed their anger and frustration at me, their new boss to-be. Some were taunting me, some were crying, and some were bitching about the new situation. It was a war zone. My two monitors served as a shallow bunker, and my only weapon was my international ETF strategy that I hadn't even traded yet. It was an ambush right in the middle of enemy territory, and I had nothing but a revolver at hand.

I knew that if I stood up and tried to take over, I would get myself "killed" right away. But it was so difficult not

The Imperial Bank, Part II

to take a chance on asserting myself since million-dollar opportunities don't come along every day. Numerous times I wanted to stand up and take over, but I resisted. I could hear senior traders yelling, "Boss, come here and take my money!"

A few seats away, one of the female managing directors, a fixed-income trader, was yelling at the mid-office IT manager, a short Indian guy, "Why the fuck is this rate curve still not implemented?"

The IT manager stood there visibly shaking, not really knowing what to do. He tried to explain it to her, but she kept screaming, "I don't care anymore. He has no risk, and he's not becoming my boss." She was obviously pissed about my situation and not her rate curve.

Sometimes during these dark days when I was struggling, I wrote Chinese calligraphy to calm my nerves. I wrote *shi nian mo yi jian*, which means *it takes ten years to forge a great sword*. I had been working on Wall Street for ten years, and after ten years of the roller-coaster ride, I thought I was finally going to get off. The calligraphy gave me strength during a very stressfully period.

Being a little bit superstitious, I kept all the pages I wrote. When I wrote a lot of them on one page, sometimes they came alive, like channeling directly with the god himself. Like complaining. Sometimes I don't know what kind of sickness or darkness I have been through so far to get this strength. My professional life was like an oscillator that lost synchronization. I either was becoming a top 500 Wall Street executive or facing doom. I was going to find ultimate happiness or complete disaster.

I didn't respond to them. I was hiding. I was passing up a promotional opportunity because I hadn't been given the right support to ensure success. William told everyone that I was going to be in charge and to report to me, and he expected me to step up and take over, but he didn't want me promoted officially. I don't know if he was trying to save money or what, but the tension was killing me. I desperately wanted the job, but I knew from past experience that leadership positions on Wall Street are suicide missions if they aren't taken at the right time. Unfortunately, by not taking over, I was almost guaranteeing my exit from the company.

Even though the traders had been informed I was in charge, nobody wanted to talk to me. The senior traders don't go to people and say, "I have problems." They have their pride and their own little worlds in which they live. If they initiated that conversation, then they would be admitting that they were under me. William conducted informal polls among the employees to see if they would support me, and the initial results were very bad. After one of these polls, he had conversations with some of the traders to see if he could convince them to support me. He got mixed results.

It wasn't long before William grew tired of the

The Imperial Bank, Part II

complaints from some of the traders, and one day he held a meeting with some of the leadership to discuss my future (or lack thereof) with the group. Everyone was discussing the meeting after they came out of the conference room, and they couldn't contain their excitement. The mood of the room switched from extreme sadness for the last couple of weeks to joy and relief. I immediately realized that I was in trouble. They sat down, and Shaun talked to Max behind my back, saying, "He's the future, but we're the past. He could write a book about how it works, but he's greedy, so he gets fired."

He knew that my knowledge and talent were worthy of the position, but he—and many others—felt I should have assumed the role of head of research and not have waited for the big payday to come. Some started to celebrate, and some of them did so with deep sarcasm, while others said, "What are you still doing here? Go cry on your mom's shoulder."

That was the toughest situation I have ever experienced. The day before, I was still dreaming of a seven-figure job, and that day I was out of the door, potentially to never find a job again. It was so gut-wrenching that I starting shaking. I could almost hear the voice in my head saying, "Get out—you screwed up." Basically I was just a notice away from getting fired. I was still doing my work at my desk, but my tears burst out a few times. I kept telling myself to never give up.

Head of Research

For a while it was as if time had stopped, as if I were in a vacuum. All of the sarcasm, laughing, and yelling were gone. I started to flash back to all of my experiences in my career and how I had come so far. I thought of all of the joy and sadness I had experienced, and I began to feel a great strength well up inside of me. It was so real that nothing outside of it mattered any more. It was almost like the world stopped existing.

I composed myself and sat at my desk. Then I heard the noise quiet down around me, this time for good. The same group of people who were so relieved and joyful just minutes before had stopped smiling. Shaun, who was sitting to my back, said to himself, "This is sick..."

I heard him start crying. And soon the sadness spread out. A couple of traders could not sit at their desks any longer. They burst into tears and rushed out of the room to gather themselves.

After a while, I approached the senior trader, Morgan, and asked if there was any more research that needed to be done. I asked in a very controlled voice since I suspected any change of pace would lead to my emotional breakdown. I looked at him and asked him quietly. He couldn't look into my eyes.

After I left, I heard him saying, "I want to fuck myself..."

Then I heard my boss comment, "He's just trying to save his job." Someone else remarked, "Maybe he believes in miracles."

The Imperial Bank, Part II

I don't know how many times I needed a miracle to survive in my career. And in the afternoon a miracle came again, because I was still there and people started to whisper, "How do you select a head of research? Tell the candidate he is fired and measure his response." William joked to another trader, "He just made himself a lot of money by almost getting himself fired."

To be promoted or not, that's the question. Soon, people started to refer to me as "God's work." Some traders started to bet whether I would get the official title or not.

Soon, summer vacations started. William went on vacation for two weeks, and on the day he left, I talked to him, and we shook hands. But to my disappointment he said nothing about the head of research position. It was confusing, because I heard Shaun say to another trader, "He works for me, but everybody works for him." But William was always cryptic.

I knew that since William was out for two weeks he had probably put me in charge. And I knew I had a big challenge ahead of me. Could I really manage this group of traders? It was do or die for me.

The next week started badly, because everyone said that I was going to be fired when William came back. But I quickly gained some momentum. I started asking people for updates on their work, and I offered encouragement to some of the traders who were making money for the company. Things started to change a little bit, and the head trader started to complain that I knew how to turn the wave of sentiment in my favor, even saying "He was *born* to be a leader."

It's somewhat challenging to talk to people you've never met and to convince them to work for you while you are technically a nobody. I tried to be nice to everyone, and I started to offer my help to try to find some common interests or collaboration. I was being careful to not upset anyone, and so things were moving slowly.

My presence certainly upset they head trader. On Wednesday, in one of my regular meetings, Derrick came in and said, "We admire your ambition in getting involved in other projects, but you seem to not be focusing on the project that you were hired for." At the end of the meeting I promised to work exclusively on my own project even though the delay in my work was mostly caused by the intraday data we had purchased and some technology issues we were experiencing. But the dressing-down was really Derrick's way of showing who was the boss.

By the end of the week I had started to refocus on my international ETF project. I was concerned, though, that if I didn't make big progress in establishing myself as a leader I might be in trouble. So the next day I wrote an e-mail to William that read, "I have been talking to a number of people within the index arbitrage group as well as outside the group for ideas, issues, or common interests.

The Imperial Bank, Part II

But my actions have caused some confusion because Derrick talked to me yesterday concerning my progress with my own project. I assured them I will work exclusively on my own project. Sorry about the confusion."

I worked a lot on my own project for the next few days, partly because my boss seemed to be demanding a lot of results, and partly because Derrick seemed to be paying close attention as well. But by the end of William's two-week vacation, I had managed to talk to more people and send another e-mail to William with some updates. Some people said that I was forcing the issue, but I had done everything by the book.

I knew, though, that I had a long way to go. A lot of people didn't hate me, but they were far from willing to work for me, maybe because they were still threatened by the fact that I would be taking over their strategies in the long run.

Usually, when I did approach William to try to open discussion about my proposed position, he would brush me off, saying "I'm three levels up…why would you talk to me?" When he was away, I was left to my own devices to raise support, but it was too difficult once the head trader and other senior people openly attacked me and refused to corporate. When William came back from vacation, I made one last attempt to communicate with him. I mentioned that I had spoken with some of the guys about interesting research projects, and he asked, "Why would you do that? I don't want you to do that. You need to focus on your own projects."

William's response sank my heart. It was worse than I had ever expected. I knew I was in deep trouble, and that afternoon I got a strange call from Shaun: "Yi, can you stop by at conference room 9A?"

I immediately realized what was going to happen. I took a deep breath, stood up, and looked one last time at my desk. Suddenly the noise of the trading floor faded far, far away. I walk toward the door, leaving behind several pages full of Chinese calligraphy that read *shi nian mo yi jian: my dream and probably my career.*

I wrote William an e-mail a few days after I was fired. I thanked him for the opportunity but explained why I didn't feel the head of research role would have worked without official support.

Four months earlier I had joined Imperial Bank hoping to find some stability in my career. I met a lot of nice and hardworking people. Unfortunately, it ended too soon for me. It was not the most disappointing experience for me, but it was certainly a dark spot on my career path. It was yet another chance at greatness that didn't come to fruition.

Sometimes my wife blames my personality for the many missteps in my career, but I ask myself, has the head of research role ever worked for someone who hadn't first established a strong track record with a group? I seemed

The Imperial Bank, Part II

crazy to some people for not wanting the job without a bump in pay, but I think I was right in assuming that it wouldn't ever work.

I certainly tried to establish myself a number of times, but with my direct bosses reminding me to focus on my own strategy and with no idea as to what to do, the end was bound to arrive sooner than later. I have been searching for myself ever since.

CHAPTER 10

The Aftermath

I walked out the door of Imperial Bank on a hot August night in 2010. I don't really remember making the trip home—the train ride, the walk home from the station—just that it was hot and muggy as I walked up the steps to my building in Jersey City. The heat pressed on my shoulders and stifled my breath. I could barely move, and I didn't really want to.

For the entire week leading up to being fired I'd fought my fate at Imperial Bank. I knew the odds were stacked against me, but I wouldn't accept the anger and shame of being fired again. It was too much to bear. I have always prided myself on staying centered and on keeping an internal balance of emotions, and in front of the other traders I had been able to do that. But standing on the street on that muggy Friday night, I felt the weight of the world pushing down on me. All I had wanted at Imperial Bank was some stability and a chance to settle down in my career. And here I was staring down uncertainty once again.

I didn't cry or throw a fit or complain about my

situation when I got in the house. I am too measured for that, and at that point I was still trying to hold on to my confidence in my abilities. It was hard, though. I was haunted by my time there both because I had a hard time accepting what had happened and because interviewing for new jobs revealed that word had gotten out. I was being followed by my failure, and every new interview brought more frustration as I tried to explain why exactly I hadn't taken the head of research job.

Initially I was completely misunderstood by people in the industry because I was seen as someone who had thrown away a prestigious position. I was questioned about my reluctance to jump into the role and why my tenure at Imperial Bank was so brief. Most people, thinking they were being polite, would whisper backhanded compliments to the other interviewers such as, "He *seems* like a nice guy," or "He has a real raw quality about him."

Through it all I tried to grin and bear it, but inside I was dying. I would say things like "It wasn't the right fit," or "I didn't receive the support I needed to assume the role," but I could see the doubt in the interviewers' eyes. They saw only what everyone else saw, an unemployed quantitative analyst/proprietary trader with a lot of experience but with not much to show for it. Inside, though, I knew I had what it takes to make it to the top. Somehow I had to let people know. But how?

The "buyers" on Wall Street, and by that I mean the

The Aftermath

employers, like to see polish in their potential employees. They want their future employees to walk in for an interview and show them a nice, steady career arc filled with consistent promotion. And here I was, showing them a roller-coaster. I was entry-level and then I was senior all in one year, and then I was gone, and they didn't understand that. I was being grilled about my experiences as though I had been reckless with my career.

Eventually the story spread among the financial industry, and soon I heard whispers in Jersey City where I and many other financial industry people live. I would go grocery shopping and overhear people talking about my story, saying, "He got greedy, and now he's gone from head of research to the end of his career." Everyone was interested in how I had almost secured a $1 million role out of "nowhere," not realizing the breadth of my experience and how hard I had worked to position myself in the market.

The looks these gossipers gave me also told me they thought I was crazy to give up the role simply because it would start without a pay increase. One day, while I was dining with my wife, I overheard another table discussing about my departure from Imperial Bank. One young woman said with a sharp voice, "How can he be so stupid? He would rather end his career than take this role without pay."

That was the first time I came close to losing my cool.

I wanted to jump up from my table and hit her in the face, but I'm not a violent person. I keep my emotions to myself, and sometimes that's a good thing when I'm in a pressure-packed situation and need to make quick decisions. The whole thing was wearing on me, however. I was so sad, and I felt hugely misunderstood and so angry.

My anger was spilling over into my home life too; while I was thrilled to be spending more time with my daughter, I was quick-tempered and prone to lashing out at her or others around me. I couldn't lash out at "luck" or "office politics" or "fate," and so I blew up at the people closest to me. The frustration of my situation hit me like a ton of bricks, and for months after the interview I carried a lot of anger and resentment about what had happened.

I have never before blamed an employer for my missing out on a job, and I am not about to. It's hard not to point fingers when you come so close to your lifelong dream and then lose it, but pointing fingers accomplishes nothing. I know that William could have handled the situation better, but ultimately I should have made my feelings clear to him when the entire idea of promotion was brought up. I have regrets, but I had always felt that failure was temporary. By the end of 2010, though, I was most definitely not as optimistic.

When your life is centered on career achievement, you start to examine yourself and your situation when things go wrong. I wondered about my future in finance and if

The Aftermath

I even had one. I thought about my approach to getting to the top and what it meant for me as a person. I don't regret jumping into the world of Wall Street or my dreams of riches; I regret just failing to achieve them so far. I don't think there's anything wrong with aspiring to greatness, and that *is* what I was doing. I have always aimed for the top in everything I've done, career especially.

When I was alone or watching my daughter at the park, I spent a lot of time thinking over my past and the countless hours I'd spent building up my skills and my expertise. Like most people on Wall Street I am an achiever by nature, always itching for new challenges and new opportunities. Sitting around my house was simply not going to work, and so I began to explore my options as a freelance consultant as I continued to look for work.

As I pushed to rebuild my career, I began to notice a shift in the way people viewed my situation. They started to comment that "Maybe he knew he couldn't survive that set of circumstances after all." I think people began to realize how desperate I was at the end at Imperial Bank and how I had fought my fate. And more and more I saw people were very emotional and sad about my story.

One day I went to gym, and as I jogged on the treadmill I overheard a young man murmuring "It's the end of his career, but at least he still has confidence." I had heard the exact same sentence two months prior but with a completely different tone, one that implied I was crazy to have walked away from the job. This young man's voice carried admiration at my resilience and my insistence on doing things the right way. He began to cry. It was more than I could take, and I lost it.

As I ran, all of the feelings of being misunderstood, of being treated unfairly, just burst out, and I started crying as well. That was the first time I had cried since leaving Imperial Bank, and four months of misunderstanding finally rushed out of my body. I let it all go, and I felt so much better for having done so. It's cathartic to cry; it offers something to the body that nothing else can, and so I cried and cried.

Over the next few weeks I was extremely emotional, as were the people I ran into who knew my story, even in public places. Sometimes I got the feeling that maybe I was delusional, because others were crying for me, even people I didn't know. I couldn't understand how people can have such strong emotions for someone they haven't met personally, but you see it all the time with celebrities. I was no celebrity, but my story was well known enough that strangers knew who I was after a while.

The emotional roller-coaster was making me highly unstable. Months of anger and frustration at being misunderstood had built up in my body, and that, coupled with the reality of the huge loss, really hit me hard. For the next few weeks, when I was alone or I heard sad music, I would cry, partly because of my personal loss but also because of

The Aftermath

the redemption I'd felt from all of the misunderstanding. Finally, people were beginning to see my side of things, and it was as if a dam had released its gate, pouring all of its contents out at once.

I am still affected by my downfall. Sometimes, while watching my daughter, a thought flashes across my mind that ignites the disappointment like a powder keg, and tears begin streaming down my face. I am fortunate that I don't need to hide my emotion from my one-year-old since she doesn't yet understand sadness. Like an angel, she dances or amuses herself with her funny gestures. Her laughter provides some happiness and joy even though I have tears in my eyes. I think watching her makes me realize that beyond career disappointments there is still so much to appreciate about life.

What I learned to appreciate about my situation in the months following the Imperial Bank job was that heroic battles are often remembered because small, outnumbered forces fight bravely in impossible battles even if they inevitably lose. I fought for what I believed in, and I knew from experience that accepting anything less than official support would have doomed me anyway. I stuck to my guns, and I lost. There was no fairytale ending for me.

Though my story has been making the rounds in the financial industry, I don't consider myself special. I am just a normal person with a very unusual experience. I can understand that some people will relate to me because I have had the ultimate strength to survive my situation. I got fired as a senior portfolio manager or as head of research, and the next week I needed to interview for a programmer's role just to extend my career, and my bravery in doing so has inspired some.

As much as I'm glad that people are seeing me in a different light, my perception of myself is independent of how people think of me. Sometimes how you feel about yourself has to come from a place beyond your role in the outside world. For me, it is the only way I can go through my roller-coaster journey.

With that inner strength I can keep cautious and motivated when I am at the top, when everyone is kissing my ass, and I also never give up fighting when I am at the bottom, when everyone is treating me like a dog. I can feel essentially the same whether I am in a million-dollar position or close to being out of the door.

CHAPTER 11

Rising from the Ashes

What do you do when you feel like you've lost it all? How do you move forward? Those are the questions I have been asking myself since August 2010. The answers haven't come easy. As much as I tried to tell myself to let go of the past, I couldn't. At least not at first. While I've always been able to quickly move on from the setbacks in my career, this time was different. The wounds to my pride and my ambitions were new and more ominous somehow than what I'd felt before, and recovery was coming slowly.

The loss of the head of research job at Imperial Bank was so profound because I was so close to it. Never before had I been as close to a job like that, and though I couldn't accept the terms under which it was offered, I never could stop myself from dreaming about the opportunities the job would bring: the corner office, the big payday, and the respect from other traders. But that was all gone, and I had to start over.

The human heart really is magic, though, and if you look deeper than its surface, you will find wonders that make the ordinary person extraordinary. Sometimes I am amazed at the strength and endurance the human spirit has for survival. I battled seriously dark emotions in the months after losing my job at Imperial Bank, and now I am preparing for a new life and whatever career opportunities come my way. I must admit that finding a positive attitude in the midst of all of my disappointment was one of the hardest transitions to make in my entire life. But now I am rising from the ashes.

The beginning of my transformation came from the same place as had the beginning of my journey to the United States: education. I wanted to stay sharp with my skills and to present interviewers with a lot of options for where to place me as an employee, so I picked up some advanced programming and derivative books. If I have to go back to being a quantitative analyst or a programmer again, then I will, and I'll do a great job at it.

I have also started exercising more. Exercise is tremendously cathartic because I believe the physical release exercise provides can act as a spiritual release as well. Running on a treadmill gives me time to think and plan for my future, a future I will make brighter than my past.

A major part of rising from the ashes has been writing this book. For me it was a very hard decision to do that. Reliving these moments has been painful and has reminded me of the struggles I've faced in my life. Aspiring to achieve lofty goals means that when you fall,

Rising from the Ashes

you fall a long way. Sometimes during my career I've felt like Icarus, flying too high, too fast. Writing this book, however, has been a chance for me to get past my failures and to help me understand what is most important about myself. I am more than my career.

For me, writing this book was also a marker in my life trajectory. It will serve as the end of one era and the beginning of the next. As I wrote each chapter, I felt myself getting stronger and stronger, almost like a cell regenerating after suffering a wound. My wound was to my heart, the very core of who I am.

I realized that a lot of people could be more successful than I have been in dollar terms, but few will experience the emotional support I have received in the months following my last job. For a short time I felt as though the people around me were breathing the same air as I was and that the world was feeling my pain.

God has tricked me time and time again and pulled me back to the ground. But Mother Earth has unselfishly cured me with her tenderness and tears. For me, the process of feeling love come back to me from the universe has been more than enough for me to restart my career. Realizing that, I become calm.

I feel as though I have reached a new stage in my personal development that I have never seen before. I feel a strength I have never felt before. And no matter what level of success I reach during the next phase of my life, I feel

I can live it with a sense of peace and contentment that I never felt on Wall Street.

I am excited, if anxious, about what my future will bring, but I know that I will get through whatever comes my way. I am a survivor, and now my ultimate challenge is to put away the burden I felt as a candidate for head of research and to restart my career. Like Rambo, I climbed back time and time again from setbacks, and now, once again, I am standing on my feet, ready to fight.

I often think about the lessons I've learned during the tumultuous years of my career and which of them might be most important to pass on to my daughter. I realized that one of the most difficult things I faced in my career was decision making under tremendous pressure. Most people face a hundred decisions a day, but those decisions are usual trivial—what to eat or which street to take to work. When you have to decide the entire course of your career, the emotions and pressures of the decision are magnified tenfold. But I have faced these decisions many times, and I have kept my head through it all. That made me special.

I want my daughter to understand that what separates a fighter from a quitter are those moments when everything is on the line. If, in those moments, she can keep her head and continue moving forward, then she will understand what I fought so hard to achieve during my time in the jungle of Wall Street.

I plan on returning stronger than ever to the job I love. I have a new sense of empowerment and personal strength that will carry me through the rest of my career, even if I have to start from scratch in a low-paying job. I look forward to the challenge, and I'm ready for the next roller-coaster ride.

Made in the USA
Lexington, KY
29 May 2011